· Cooking for Today ·

CARIBBEAN COOKING

·Cooking for Today·

CARIBBEAN COOKING

JANE HARTSHORN

First published in Great Britain in 1996 by
Parragon Book Service Ltd
Unit 13–17
Avonbridge Trading Estate
Atlantic Road
Avonmouth
Bristol BS11 9QD

ISBN 0-7525-1805-4

Produced by Haldane Mason, London

Printed in Italy

Acknowledgements:
Art Direction: Ron Samuels
Editor: Vicky Hanson
Series Design: Pedro & Frances Prá-Lopez/Kingfisher Design, London
Page Design: Somewhere Creative
Photography and Styling: Patrick McLeavey
Home Economist: Jane Hartshorn

Photographs on pages 20 and 62 reproduced by permission of
ZEFA Picture Library (UK) Ltd
Photographs on pages 6, 34 and 48 reproduced by permission of Diana Vowles

Note:
Cup measurements in this book are for American cups. Tablespoons are assumed to be 15 ml.
Unless otherwise stated, milk is assumed to be full-fat, eggs are standard size 2
and pepper is freshly ground black pepper.

Author's acknowledgements:
I would like to thank the following people for all their help during the writing of this book: Faye Padden, Julia Hartshorn, Emma and Jim McClure, Judy Robinson, Enid Davis, Christopher and Christine Cole, Michael Ritte, Benkole Adeniji, Calvin Robinson, Allison Hartshorn, Yemisi Adeniji, Linda Bell, and my parents Eleanor and Colin Hartshorn.

Contents

CHAPTER ONE

Soups & Appetizers

All the ingredients for tasty appetizers are abundant in the Caribbean; fresh fish and shellfish, unusual and exotic vegetables, and an array of herbs and spices. Many of the more popular appetizers often appear at other times of the day as well. Dishes such as Plantain & Breadfruit Crisps (see page 16) and Cornmeal & Seafood Parcels (see page 13) may be served for breakfast, lunch or supper.

It is quite common in the Caribbean kitchen for nothing to go to waste, and surplus ingredients form the basis for the rich homemade stock that gives soups their excellent flavour. Soups are usually thick, rich and hearty and make a substantial main meal as well as an appetizer. Cornmeal dumplings are traditionally added to soups, along with island vegetables such as cho-cho, callaloo, pumpkin, plantain and yam, plus any other ingredients which might be at hand.

Soups and appetizers are the ideal dishes to begin a Caribbean-style meal and give a taste of what is to come.

Opposite: *A peanut vendor peddles his wares in Port of Spain, Trinidad.*

STEP 1

STEP 2

STEP 3

STEP 4

PEPPERPOT SOUP

A filling soup which can be found on several of the islands. It is often confused with another dish called Pepperpot, which is a stew from Guyana. This soup is best made the day before it is to be served, as it improves with keeping.

SERVES 6–8

500 g/1 lb shin of beef, cubed
250 g/8 oz salt beef, cubed
500 g/1 lb callaloo, trimmed and chopped
2 onions, chopped finely
2 garlic cloves, crushed
4 spring onions (scallions), chopped
1 tsp dried thyme
1 fresh green chilli
250 g/8 oz yam, sliced
250 g/8 oz coco, sliced
250 g/8 oz unshelled raw prawns (shrimp)
1 litre/1³/₄ pints/4¹/₂ cups beef stock
15 g/¹/₂ oz/1 tbsp unsalted butter
125 g/4 oz okra, trimmed and sliced finely
salt and pepper

1 Put the beef and salt beef into a large saucepan, pour over enough cold water to cover, and bring to the boil. Reduce the heat, cover and simmer for 1¹/₂ hours.

2 Put the callaloo in another saucepan and cover with cold water. Bring to the boil. Cook for 10 minutes, drain and purée in a food processor or blender for 30 seconds, or press through a sieve (strainer).

3 Add the callaloo purée, onions, garlic, spring onions (scallions), thyme, chilli, yam, coco, prawns (shrimp) and seasoning to the meat. Add the stock and bring to the boil, then simmer for 20 minutes, until the coco and yam are soft.

4 Melt the butter in a small frying pan (skillet) and fry the okra until golden brown. Add to the soup and cook for a further 5 minutes.

5 Discard the chilli, pour the soup into warm soup bowls or a tureen and serve.

VARIATIONS

Coco is very similar to potato, so you could use potatoes if coco is not available. Alternatively double the quantity of yam.
  Cornmeal dumplings (see page 79) may be added to the soup for the last 15 minutes of cooking.

STEP 1

STEP 2

STEP 3

STEP 4

CALLALOO

This is probably the most famous of all the island soups, and each island has its own variation. The main ingredients are callaloo, okra, coconut, pork and crab meat. This particular recipe is Trinidadian with a St Lucian twist.

SERVES 6–8

30 g/1 oz/2 tbsp butter
125 g/4 oz salt pork, cubed
1 onion or 4 spring onions (scallions),
    chopped
1 garlic clove, crushed
1 celery stick, sliced
250 g/8 oz callaloo, shredded
1 sprig fresh thyme
1.25 litres/2¼ pints/5½ cups chicken stock
    or water
5 cm/2 inch piece creamed coconut, chopped
175 g/6 oz/¾ cup white crab meat,
    shredded
125 g/4 oz okra, sliced
West Indian hot pepper sauce (optional)
salt and pepper
bread to serve

1 Melt the butter in a frying pan (skillet) and gently fry the salt pork for 2–3 minutes.

2 Add the onions or spring onions (scallions) and garlic and fry until soft and golden. Transfer to a saucepan.

3 Stir in the celery, callaloo, thyme, stock or water and coconut. Bring to the boil, cover, reduce the heat and simmer for 10 minutes.

4 Add the crab meat and okra and simmer, covered, for a further 10 minutes. Season to taste and add a dash of West Indian hot pepper sauce if liked. Serve with bread.

CRAB MEAT

Fresh, canned or frozen crab meat (frozen meat must be defrosted before using) can be used quite successfully in this soup. Crab claws or crab meat in the shells may be used for a more authentic soup.

CALLALOO

Callaloo may be replaced by most green leaves, including spinach, the green part of Swiss chard, Chinese spinach or finely shredded greens. Callaloo is also available in cans from West Indian shops.

CORNMEAL & SEAFOOD PARCELS

These banana-leaf parcels are a national favourite in Trinidad and the whole family is often involved in making them. They are usually eaten as an appetizer or snack, or for breakfast with hot pepper sauce.

STEP 1

MAKES 18

2 tbsp sunflower oil
1 onion, chopped finely
1 garlic clove, crushed
1 fresh red chilli, chopped
2 tomatoes, skinned and chopped
1 small red (bell) pepper, chopped finely
2 tbsp capers, chopped
250 g/8 oz/1⅓ cups peeled cooked prawns
 (shrimp)
250 g/8 oz/1 cup white crab meat, shredded
1 tbsp finely chopped fresh chives
1 tsp finely grated ginger root
1 tsp chopped fresh coriander (cilantro)
pared rind of 1 lime
salt and pepper

CORNMEAL WRAPPERS:
500 g/1 lb/3 cups coarse cornmeal
30 g/1 oz/2 tbsp margarine, diced
5 tbsp sunflower oil
2 tsp salt
650 ml/22 fl oz/2¾ cups boiling water
3–4 banana leaves

1 Heat the oil in a frying pan (skillet) and gently fry the onion until soft. Stir in the garlic and chilli and cook for 3 minutes. Stir in the tomatoes, red (bell) pepper, capers, prawns (shrimp), crab meat, chives, ginger and coriander (cilantro) and cook for 1–2 minutes. Add the lime rind, season and leave to cool.

2 To make the cornmeal wrappers, place the cornmeal in a bowl, add the margarine and rub in with 2 tablespoons of the oil and the salt. Add the boiling water and mix well to make a smooth dough. Roll into 18 balls.

3 Cut the banana leaves into 36 rectangles, 20 x 25 cm/8 x 10 inches. Place in a bowl and pour over the boiling water. Drain and refresh under cold water. Pat dry with paper towels.

4 Brush a leaf with a little of the remaining oil. Place a cornmeal ball in the centre and pat down to form a circle about 5 mm/¼ inch thick. Spread 1½ tablespoons of filling in the centre.

5 Fold half the leaf over the filling, then fold over the other half. Fold in the ends to make a parcel. Place the parcel folded side down on a second leaf, on the opposite grain, and repeat the folding to enclose it. Secure with string.

6 Repeat to make 18 parcels. Place in a large saucepan of boiling salted water and simmer for 1 hour. Drain the parcels and serve.

STEP 2

STEP 4

STEP 5

STEP 1

STEP 3

STEP 4

STEP 5

CRAB & POTATO BALLS

These make an unusual first course. They are very popular in the Dominican Republic, where they may also be made with chopped prawns (shrimp). Serve them with a rich tomato sauce, if you like.

MAKES 30

500 g/1 lb potatoes, cut into chunks
45 g/1½ oz/3 tbsp butter
2 egg yolks
60 g/2 oz/½ cup Edam cheese, grated
1 tbsp finely chopped fresh flat-leaf parsley
1 onion, chopped finely
500 g/1 lb/2 cups crab meat, shredded
plain (all-purpose) flour for coating
1 egg, beaten
60 g/2 oz/½ cup dry white breadcrumbs
oil for deep-frying
salt and pepper

TO GARNISH:
lemon or lime wedges
spinach leaves

1 Cook the potatoes in boiling salted water until tender. Drain and mash with 30 g/1 oz/2 tablespoons of the butter, the egg yolks, cheese, parsley and seasoning. Set aside.

2 Heat the remaining butter in a small frying pan (skillet) and gently fry the onion until soft but not brown. Transfer to a bowl and leave to cool.

3 Add the crab meat and mashed potato to the onion and combine

well. Form into 30 small balls. Place on a baking sheet lined with baking parchment and refrigerate for at least 30 minutes.

4 Roll the balls in the flour, dip in the beaten egg and then coat with the breadcrumbs.

5 Half fill a deep-fat fryer or saucepan with oil and heat to 190°C/375°F, or until a cube of bread turns brown in 40 seconds. Deep fry the balls in batches for 5–6 minutes until golden brown all over. Remove with a perforated spoon and drain on paper towels. Keep warm until all the balls have been cooked.

6 Serve garnished with lemon or lime wedges and spinach leaves.

PARTY FOOD

The balls are good for entertaining as they can be made ahead of time: keep refrigerated at step 3 until ready to fry.

If the balls are made a smaller size, they can be served on cocktail sticks.

STEP 1

STEP 2

STEP 3

STEP 5

PLANTAIN & BREADFRUIT CRISPS WITH AVOCADO DIP

These crisps are very popular at parties; they are served on their own or with a dip such as this creamy avocado one.

SERVES 4–6

1 breadfruit
1 green plantain
soya oil for deep frying
coarse sea salt

AVOCADO DIP:
1 large ripe avocado
2 tsp lime juice
1 garlic clove, crushed
2 tsp finely chopped spring onion (scallion)
90 g/ 3 oz/¹/₃ cup full-fat soft cheese, softened
1 tbsp coconut milk
pinch of chilli powder
dash of West Indian hot pepper sauce
salt and pepper

TO GARNISH:
spring onion (scallion) slices
chilli powder

1 Peel the breadfruit and cut into quarters. Cook in boiling salted water for 20 minutes until just tender. Dry on paper towels then slice thinly.

2 Peel the plantain and slice very thinly.

3 Half fill a deep-fat fryer or saucepan with oil and heat to 190°C/375°F or until a cube of bread turns brown in 40 seconds. Deep fry the plantain and breadfruit slices in batches for 2–3 minutes until crisp and golden. Remove with a perforated spoon and drain on paper towels. Sprinkle with salt and leave to cool.

4 To make the avocado dip, peel the avocado and mash the flesh with a fork or blend in a food processor until smooth.

5 Mix in the lime juice, garlic, spring onion (scallion), soft cheese, coconut milk, chilli powder and pepper sauce. Season to taste.

6 Garnish the dip with spring onions (scallions) and chilli powder and serve with the crisps.

AVOCADO DIP

The avocado dip may be made a few hours in advance. To stop it from discolouring, immerse the stone (pit) into the mixture. Remember to remove the stone (pit) before serving.

STEP 1

STEP 2

STEP 3

STEP 4

CHORIZO, CORIANDER (CILANTRO) & GINGER FRITTERS

Known as fritters in the English-speaking islands, 'beignets' in French, and 'frituras' in Spanish, these deep-fried morsels are very popular. Each cook may add different ingredients, depending on availability.

MAKES 20–24

125 g/4 oz/1 cup plain (all-purpose) flour
1½ tsp baking powder
4 eggs
2 tsp melted unsalted butter
2 tsp corn or groundnut oil
2 tsp white rum
90 g/3 oz chorizo sausage, chopped
2 tsp chopped fresh coriander (cilantro)
1 tsp finely grated ginger root
corn or groundnut oil for deep frying
salt and pepper
sprigs of fresh coriander (cilantro) to
  garnish
West Indian hot pepper sauce to serve

1 Sift the flour and baking powder into a bowl.

2 Make a well in the centre and add the eggs, butter, oil and rum and beat until the batter is smooth. Leave to stand for 1 hour.

3 Stir in the chorizo sausage, chopped coriander (cilantro), ginger and seasoning.

4 Half fill a deep-fat fryer or saucepan with oil and heat to 190°C/375°F, or until a teaspoon of the batter sizzles on contact. Drop tablespoons of the batter into the oil and deep fry for 6–8 minutes until golden brown all over. Remove with a perforated spoon and drain on paper towels.

5 Serve garnished with sprigs of coriander (cilantro) and with hot pepper sauce for dipping.

SHALLOW FRYING

These fritters may also be shallow fried in about 5 cm/2 inches of oil. Heat the oil then fry the fritters for 2–3 minutes on each side until golden brown.

CHORIZO SAUSAGE

Chorizo is a Spanish sausage. It is lightly smoked and made from coarsely chopped pork seasoned with chilli pepper and garlic. It is available from supermarkets and delicatessens. Italian sausage, garlic sausage or smoked ham make good alternatives.

CHAPTER TWO

Fish & Shellfish

When you think of the Caribbean you often think of seafood, which is a hallmark of Caribbean food. The warm waters of the Caribbean are ideal for ensuring a plentiful supply of fish and shellfish. When the catch arrives on the islands it provides a colourful display of quite astonishing fish — flying fish, barracuda, crayfish, crab and red snapper are just a few of those available. Despite the abundance of fresh fish, salt cod is also still popular and has a distinctive flavour that is essential to many traditional island recipes.

It is difficult to be specific about the fish used in recipes: the same fish may have a different name on different islands and the name may even vary within the same island. If you have trouble getting hold of a particular fish, another type may be substituted; if the recipe is followed in other respects the flavour will still be authentic.

Shellfish is widely used in recipes and is best straight from the sea. Most of the shellfish are quite familiar, such as prawns (shrimp), crayfish, crab and lobster.

Opposite: Fish dishes play an important role in the cuisine of all island communities, but the tropical waters of the Caribbean offer a particularly rich supply.

STEP 1

STEP 2

STEP 3

STEP 4

SALT FISH & ACKEE

This is often regarded as the national dish of Jamaica. It can be served at breakfast, as an appetizer or as a main course, and is traditionally accompanied by fried plantain and Rice & Peas (see page 54).

SERVES 4–6

250 g/8 oz salt cod, soaked overnight
30 g/1oz/2 tbsp butter
2 tbsp olive oil
2 slices streaky bacon, chopped
4 spring onions (scallions), sliced
1 onion, sliced
¹/₂ tsp dried thyme
2 fresh green chillies, sliced finely
1 green (bell) pepper, sliced
2 tomatoes, skinned and chopped
350 g/12 oz can ackee, drained
pepper

FRIED PLANTAIN:
30 g/1 oz/2 tbsp butter
2 ripe plantains, sliced lengthways

1 Drain the salt cod and rinse under cold water. Put in a saucepan, cover with cold water and bring to the boil. Cover and simmer for 10 minutes. Drain, rinse and remove the skin and bones and flake the flesh.

2 Heat the butter with the oil in a frying pan (skillet), add the bacon and fry for 5 minutes until crisp. Remove with a perforated spoon and drain on paper towels.

3 Fry the spring onions (scallions), onion, thyme, chillies and (bell) pepper for 5 minutes. Add the tomatoes and cook for a further 5 minutes.

4 Stir in the salt cod, ackee and bacon and cook for a further 2–3 minutes.

5 Meanwhile, make the fried plantain. Heat the butter in a frying pan (skillet) and cook the plantains for 2–3 minutes per side. Drain on paper towels and serve with the cod and ackee.

ACKEE

For convenience, this recipe uses canned ackee, which is available from West Indian stores and markets. The skin, seeds and membrane of fresh ackee are poisonous. The fruit must also be eaten only when just ripe, as both unripe and overripe ackee are poisonous.

STEP 3

STEP 4

STEP 5

STEP 6

SALT-FISH FRITTERS WITH SEAFOOD SAUCE

Each island has its own name and recipe for these delectable fritters.
This particular recipe is for the Jamaican 'Stamp and Go'.

MAKES 24

250 g/8 oz salt cod, soaked overnight
125 g/4 oz/1 cup plain (all-purpose) flour
1 tsp baking powder
1/2 tsp salt
1 egg, lightly beaten
180 ml/6 fl oz/3/4 cup milk
15 g/1/2 oz/1 tbsp butter, melted
1 onion, grated finely
1 fresh red chilli, chopped finely
corn oil, for frying

SEAFOOD SAUCE:
150 ml/1/4 pint/2/3 cup mayonnaise
2 tbsp tomato purée (paste)
1/2 tsp chilli powder
1 tbsp lemon juice
1 tsp wholegrain mustard

TO GARNISH:
chilli powder
basil sprigs
chicory (endive) leaves

1 Drain the salt cod and rinse under cold water. Put in a saucepan, cover with cold water and bring to the boil. Cover and simmer for 10 minutes.

2 Drain, rinse and remove the skin and bones and flake the flesh.

3 Mix together the flour, baking powder and salt. Make a well in the centre and pour in the egg, milk and butter. Mix to a smooth batter. Stir in the onion, chilli and salt cod.

4 Heat about 1 cm/1/2 inch of oil in a large deep frying pan (skillet). Drop tablespoons of the mixture, spaced well apart, into the oil and fry for 3–4 minutes until golden on one side.

5 Turn over the fritters and cook for a further 3–4 minutes until the second side is golden. Remove and drain on paper towels. Keep warm. Repeat with the remaining batter.

6 To make the seafood sauce, mix together the mayonnaise, tomato purée (paste), chilli powder, lemon juice and mustard.

7 Serve the fritters with the sauce, garnished with chilli powder, basil sprigs and chicory (endive) leaves.

ESCOVITCH FISH

This famous Jamaican dish was introduced to the Caribbean by the Spanish – escovitch means 'pickled'.

STEP 1

Serves 4

4 red snapper, scaled
juice of 1 lime
3 green (bell) peppers, sliced
2 onions, sliced
3 carrots, cut into matchsticks
1 fresh bay leaf
1 tbsp finely chopped ginger root
6 black peppercorns
pinch of ground mace
500 ml/ 16 fl oz/ 2 cups water
5 tbsp olive oil
6 tbsp malt or white wine vinegar
salt and pepper

DUMPLINGS:
250 g/ 8 oz/ 2 cups self-raising flour
pinch of salt
cold water
oil for frying

TO GARNISH:
pimento-stuffed olives, sliced
lime wedges
sprigs of fresh parsley

1 Put the fish in a shallow non-metallic dish or dishes and season with salt, pepper and lime juice. Leave for 20 minutes.

2 Place the (bell) peppers, onions, carrots, bay leaf, ginger, peppercorns, mace, water and salt in a saucepan. Cover and simmer for 30 minutes.

3 Add 2 tablespoons of the olive oil and the vinegar and simmer for a further 1–2 minutes.

4 Heat the remaining oil in a large frying pan (skillet) and fry the fish in batches for 6–8 minutes on each side. Transfer to a serving dish.

5 Meanwhile, make the dumplings. Sift the flour and salt into a bowl. Add enough cold water to make a soft dough. Knead lightly, shape into balls and flatten.

6 Heat 1 cm/½ inch oil in a frying pan (skillet). Fry the dumplings in batches for 3–4 minutes on each side, until golden. Remove with a perforated spoon and drain on paper towels. Keep warm while frying the remainder.

7 Pour the sauce over the fish, garnish with olives, lime wedges and parsley and serve with the dumplings.

STEP 2

STEP 3

STEP 4

SEA BREAM & SWEET POTATO PIE

*This is a fish pie with a difference – a creamy fish sauce topped with
golden sweet potatoes for a substantial supper-time meal.*

STEP 1

STEP 3

STEP 4

STEP 5

SERVES 6

15 g/¹/₂ oz/1 tbsp butter
3 tbsp groundnut oil
250 g/8 oz sweet potatoes, unpeeled, sliced
   thinly
1 onion, chopped finely
750 g/1¹/₂ lb sea bream fillets, skinned and
   cut into large pieces
2 hard-boiled (hard-cooked) eggs, chopped
sprigs of fresh parsley to garnish

CURRY SAUCE:
45 g/1¹/₂ oz/3 tbsp butter
2 tbsp plain (all-purpose) flour
300 ml/¹/₂ pint/1¹/₄ cups milk
90 g/3 oz/³/₄ cup mature (sharp) Cheddar
   cheese, grated
1 tsp curry powder
2 tbsp chopped fresh flat-leaf parsley
salt and pepper

1 Melt the butter with 2 tablespoons
of the oil in a frying pan (skillet).
Fry the sweet potatoes in batches for 1–2
minutes on each side, without allowing
to soften. Remove with a perforated
spoon and drain on paper towels.

2 Add the onion to the pan and fry
for 5 minutes. Add the sea bream
and cook for a further 5 minutes.

3 Remove the pan from the heat and
stir in the eggs. Transfer the fish
mixture to an ovenproof dish.

4 To make the sauce, melt the butter
in a saucepan, add the flour and
stir over a low heat for 1–2 minutes.
Remove from the heat and gradually
stir in the milk. Return to the heat and
stir for a further 2–3 minutes. Add two-
thirds of the cheese, the curry powder,
parsley and seasoning.

5 Pour the sauce over the fish and
mix gently. Layer the sweet potato
over the top, overlapping the slices.
Brush with the remaining oil and
sprinkle with the remaining cheese. Bake
in a preheated oven at 180°C/350°F/Gas
Mark 4 for 30 minutes until golden.
Garnish with parsley and serve.

VARIATION

Alternate the slices of sweet potato with
ordinary potatoes for an unusual contrast
of flavours and colours.

STEP 1

STEP 2

STEP 3

STEP 4

RED MULLET & COCONUT LOAF WITH PEPPER SAUCE

This fish and coconut loaf is ideal to take along on picnics, as it can be served cold as well as hot.

SERVES 4–6

250 g/8 oz red mullet fillets, skinned
2 small tomatoes, deseeded and chopped finely
2 green (bell) peppers, chopped finely
1 onion, chopped finely
1 fresh red chilli, chopped finely
150 g/5 oz/2¹⁄₂ cups breadcrumbs
600 ml/1 pint/2¹⁄₂ cups coconut liquid
salt and pepper

HOT PEPPER SAUCE:
120 ml/4 fl oz/¹⁄₂ cup tomato ketchup
1 tsp West Indian hot pepper sauce
¹⁄₄ tsp hot mustard

TO GARNISH:
lemon twists
sprigs of fresh chervil

1 Finely chop the fish and mix with the tomatoes, (bell) peppers, onion and chilli.

2 Stir in the breadcrumbs, coconut liquid and seasoning.

3 Grease and base-line a 500 g/1 lb loaf tin (pan) and add the fish. Bake in a preheated oven at 200°C/400°F/Gas Mark 6 for 1–1¹⁄₄ hours until set.

4 To make the hot pepper sauce, mix together the tomato ketchup, hot pepper sauce and mustard until smooth and creamy.

5 To serve, cut the loaf into slices, garnish with lemon twists and chervil and serve hot or cold with the hot pepper sauce.

COCONUT LIQUID

Coconut liquid is the juice found inside a coconut. Use a hammer and screwdriver or the tip of a sturdy knife to poke out the three 'eyes' in the top of the coconut and pour out the liquid.

CHILLIES

Be careful when preparing chillies because the juices can irritate the skin, especially the face. Wash your hands after handling them or wear clean rubber gloves to prepare them if preferred.

The seeds of the chilli are very hot, so after slitting the chilli, rinse it out well to remove all the seeds.

STEP 1

STEP 2

STEP 3

STEP 4

STUFFED BAKED CRAB

This dish makes an impressive appetizer at a dinner party; choose small crabs so each guest can have their own individual serving.

SERVES 4

4 small cooked crabs, weighing about
   350 g/12 oz each
90 g/3 oz/1½ cups fresh breadcrumbs
1 fresh red chilli, preferably Scotch bonnet,
   deseeded and chopped finely
3 tbsp chopped fresh chives
2 tbsp chopped fresh parsley
2 garlic cloves, crushed
1 tbsp lemon juice
¼ tsp ground allspice
3 tbsp dark rum or Madeira
45 g/1½ oz/⅓ cup grated Parmesan cheese
15 g/½ oz/1 tbsp butter
salt and pepper
green salad to serve

TO GARNISH:
lime wedges
fresh chives

1 Pull away the 2 flaps between the large claws of the crab, stand it upside down where the flaps were and bang down firmly on the rounded end with the heel of your hand.

2 Separate the crab from its top shell. Remove the mouth and the stomach sac, which lies immediately below the mouth, and discard.

3 Pull out the feathery gills and discard. Scrape out the brown and white meat from both sides of the shell and reserve. Crack the claws using a rolling pin and remove the meat. Scrub the shells.

4 Finely chop the crab meat and mix with 60 g/2 oz/1 cup of the breadcrumbs, the chilli, chives, parsley, garlic, lemon juice, allspice, rum or Madeira and seasoning.

5 Spoon the crab mixture back into the shells. Sprinkle with the remaining breadcrumbs mixed with the cheese. Dot with butter and bake in a preheated oven at 180°C/350°F/Gas Mark 4 for 25–30 minutes until golden brown. Garnish with lime wedges and chives and serve with a green salad.

FRESH CRAB

If fresh crabs are not available use fresh, frozen or canned crab meat and bake in ramekin dishes or scallop shells.

CHAPTER THREE

Meat & Poultry

The Spanish were responsible for introducing livestock to the Caribbean. Since then, meat and poultry have become an integral part of all West Indian cuisine. Popular forms of meat on most of the islands include goat, chicken, mutton and pork. Salt beef and salt pork also appear in many traditional West Indian meat dishes.

Meat and poultry are often 'jerked' – marinated or highly seasoned during cooking – which is an essential technique of Caribbean cuisine. The main ingredients of the seasoning are herbs, onion, chives and garlic, with additional ingredients added according to each individual recipe or the local availability of herbs and spices. Whatever the ingredients, it is this seasoning and method of cooking that give West Indian meat and poultry dishes their unique flavour.

Opposite: *Stunning costumes on display at mardi gras – carnival time.*

STEP 1

STEP 2

STEP 3

STEP 4

JERK CHICKEN

Rubbing pastes and 'rubs' into meat, poultry, fish or seafood – an old method of cooking that was introduced by the Arawak Indians – helps to tenderize the meat. The technique is still as popular as ever on all the Caribbean islands.

SERVES 6

1.5 kg/ 3 lb chicken pieces
cherry tomatoes to garnish
salad to serve

MARINADE:
6 spring onions (scallions)
2 fresh red chillies, preferably Scotch bonnet
2 tbsp dark soy sauce
2 tbsp lime juice
3 tsp ground allspice
$^{1}/_{2}$ tsp ground bay leaves
1 tsp ground cinnamon
2 garlic cloves, chopped
2 tsp brown sugar
1 tsp dried thyme
$^{1}/_{2}$ tsp salt

1 To make the marinade, chop the spring onions (scallions). Deseed and finely chop the chillies.

2 Put the spring onions (scallions), chillies, soy sauce, lime juice, allspice, ground bay leaves, cinnamon, garlic, sugar, thyme and salt in a food processor or blender and blend until smooth. Alternatively, finely chop the spring onions (scallions) and chillies, add to the remaining ingredients and, using a pestle and mortar, work to a paste.

3 Place the chicken in a shallow dish and spoon over the marinade. Cover and refrigerate for 24 hours, turning the chicken several times.

4 Brush a grill (broiler) rack with oil and place the chicken on it. Grill (broil) under a preheated medium grill (broiler) for about 15–20 minutes on each side until the chicken juices run clear when the thickest part of each piece is pierced with a sharp knife.

5 Garnish with cherry tomatoes and serve with a salad.

VARIATIONS

Use pork chops, or a joint of pork that can be roasted in the oven. Firm fish such as red snapper, red mullet or sea bass may also be used for this recipe. Remove any scales before marinating.

BARBECUE

When the weather is fine, cook the chicken over a barbecue for a more authentic flavour.

CHICKEN WITH RICE & PEAS

This dish, which is also known as chicken pelau, is a national favourite in Trinidad and Tobago. The secret of a good pelau is that it must be brown in colour, which is achieved by caramelizing the chicken first.

STEP 2

SERVES 6

1 onion, chopped
2 garlic cloves
1 tbsp chopped fresh chives
1 tbsp chopped fresh thyme
2 celery sticks with leaves, chopped
350 ml/12 fl oz/1¹/₂ cups water
¹/₂ fresh coconut, chopped
liquid from 1 fresh coconut
500 g/16 oz can pigeon peas, drained
1 fresh red chilli, deseeded and cut into strips
2 tbsp groundnut oil
2 tbsp caster (superfine) sugar
1.5 kg/3 lb chicken pieces
250 g/8 oz/generous 1 cup long-grain rice,
   rinsed and drained
salt and pepper
celery leaves to garnish

1 Put the onion, garlic, chives, thyme, celery and 4 tablespoons of the water into a food processor or blender and blend until smooth. Alternatively, chop the onion and celery very finely, then grind with the garlic and herbs in a pestle and mortar, gradually mixing in the water. Pour into a pan and set aside.

2 Put the chopped coconut and liquid into the food processor or blender and mix to a thick milk, adding

STEP 4

water if necessary. Alternatively, finely grate the coconut and mix with the liquid. Add to the onion and celery mixture in the pan.

3 Stir in the pigeon peas and chilli and cook over a low heat for 15 minutes. Season to taste.

4 Put the oil and sugar in a heavy-based saucepan or flameproof casserole and cook over a moderate heat until the sugar begins to caramelize.

5 Add the chicken and cook for 15–20 minutes, turning frequently, until browned all over.

6 Stir in the coconut mixture, the rice and remaining water. Bring to the boil, then reduce the heat, cover and simmer for 20 minutes until the chicken and rice are tender and the liquid has been absorbed. Garnish with celery leaves and serve.

STEP 5

STEP 6

STEP 1

STEP 2

STEP 3

STEP 4

CURRIED LAMB

This dish is traditionally made with goat, but lamb is used here because it is more widely available. If you are lucky enough to obtain goat, cook it in exactly the same way. This dish is popular in Jamaica and many of the English-speaking islands.

SERVES 6

2–3 tbsp corn or groundnut oil
1.5 kg/3 lb lean boneless lamb, cut into
*   5 cm/2 inch cubes*
2 large onions, chopped
2 fresh red chillies, sliced (optional)
3 tbsp mild or hot curry powder
300 ml/¹/₂ pint/1¹/₄ cups coconut milk
1 fresh bay leaf
¹/₂ tsp ground allspice
300 ml/¹/₂ pint/1¹/₄ cups lamb or chicken
*   stock*
2 tbsp lime or lemon juice
salt and pepper

TO GARNISH:
lime rind
fresh red chillies

TO SERVE:
rice or roti
banana leaves (optional)

1 Heat the oil in a frying pan (skillet) and fry the lamb until brown. Remove with a perforated spoon and place in a large flameproof casserole.

2 Fry the onions and chillies, if using, in the frying pan (skillet) until golden brown.

3 Add the curry powder and cook for a further 2–3 minutes, stirring.

4 Add the fried onion to the casserole with the coconut milk, bay leaf, allspice, seasoning and just enough stock to barely cover the meat. Cover and simmer for 2 hours until the lamb is tender.

5 Just before serving, add the lime or lemon juice and cook for a further 2–3 minutes. Garnish with lime rind and chillies and serve on banana leaves, if liked, with rice or roti.

ROTI

Roti is a flat Indian-style bread that can sometimes be found in supermarkets and West Indian stores. This curry is sometimes served spooned into the centre of a large roti, which is then folded over the filling like an envelope. It can be eaten with a knife and fork; fingers, however, are more fun.

STEP 1

STEP 2

STEP 4

STEP 5

LAMB KEBABS WITH YARD-LONG BEANS

This dish originated in Aruba, but kebabs or skewered meats are popular all over the Caribbean and are often cooked over a barbecue.

SERVES 4

2 tbsp grated onion
1 tbsp hot paprika
1 tbsp grated ginger root
2 garlic cloves, crushed
1 tbsp curry powder
6 tbsp lime juice
3 tbsp peanut oil
1 kg/2 lb lean lamb, cubed
16 pickling onions
8 slices streaky bacon, halved
2 red (bell) peppers, cut into 16 squares
16 cherry tomatoes
4 yard-long beans, parboiled for 1–2
  minutes
salt and pepper
rice to serve

1 In a large bowl, mix the onion, paprika, ginger, garlic, curry powder, lime juice, oil and seasoning. Stir in the lamb, cover and refrigerate for at least 2 hours, or overnight.

2 Cover the onions with boiling water and leave for 5 minutes. Drain, leave to cool, then peel.

3 Wrap a piece of bacon around each (bell) pepper square.

4 Lift the lamb from the marinade, reserving the marinade. Thread the lamb, onions, bacon and (bell) pepper squares and tomatoes alternately on to 4 long skewers.

5 Wrap the beans around the skewers, securing in place with string. Brush on all sides with the marinade.

6 Cook the kebabs under a preheated medium grill (broiler) for 10–15 minutes, turning and brushing them frequently with the marinade, until the lamb is cooked.

7 Discard the string and serve the kebabs with rice.

YARD-LONG BEANS

These beans can sometimes be found in shops selling oriental foods. If they are unavailable, use strips of spring onions (scallions) or runner (green) beans and secure in place with wooden cocktail sticks (toothpicks) if necessary.

STEP 1

STEP 2

STEP 3

STEP 4

SANCOCHE

*This traditional Trinidadian plantation stew is sometimes served as a
soup. It has humble beginnings but certainly makes a filling,
flavoursome one-pot meal.*

SERVES 6

250 g/8 oz salt beef, cubed
250 g/8 oz salt pork, cubed
4–5 tbsp oil
275 g/9 oz stewing beef, cubed
2 onions, chopped
250 g/8 oz red lentils or split peas, rinsed
600 ml/1 pint/2½ cups boiling water
250 g/8 oz green bananas, sliced thickly
250 g/8 oz yam, sliced thickly
250 g/8 oz sweet potatoes, sliced thickly
125 g/4 oz okra, trimmed
1 fresh red chilli
salt and pepper

1 Place the salt beef and salt pork in a large bowl. Pour over enough cold water to cover and leave to soak for 1 hour. Drain and pat the meat dry with paper towels.

2 Heat 2 tablespoons of the oil in a large deep saucepan or flameproof casserole and fry the salt beef for 6–8 minutes until brown on all sides. Remove with a perforated spoon and transfer to a plate. Add the salt pork and stewing beef to the pan and cook until browned, adding more oil if necessary. Remove with a perforated spoon.

3 Add the onions and cook for 5 minutes. Return the meat to the pan, add the lentils or split peas and pour over the boiling water. Bring to the boil. Reduce the heat, cover and simmer for 1½ hours.

4 Add the green bananas, yam, sweet potatoes, okra, chilli and seasoning. Cook for a further 25–30 minutes.

5 To serve, discard the chilli and transfer to a warmed serving dish.

VARIATION

Use unsalted pork and beef if you cannot find the salted versions.

STUFFED PAW-PAWS (PAPAYAS)

This dish would traditionally be made with green or unripe paw-paws (papayas) which are used as a vegetable in the Caribbean. In this recipe they are ripe, however, providing a sweet contrast to the filling.

STEP 1

SERVES 4

2 tbsp oil
6 spring onions (scallions), sliced
1 garlic clove, crushed
300 g/10 oz/1¼ cups minced (ground) beef
1 fresh red chilli, chopped finely
2 ripe tomatoes, skinned and chopped
2 tbsp sultanas (golden raisins)
1 tbsp cashew nuts, toasted and chopped
2 tbsp freshly grated Parmesan cheese
2 ripe but firm paw-paws (papayas), halved
    lengthways and deseeded
1 tbsp fine fresh breadcrumbs
salt and pepper
sprigs of fresh flat-leaf parsley to garnish

1 Heat the oil in a frying pan (skillet), add the spring onions (scallions) and cook for 5 minutes until soft. Add the garlic and cook for 2 minutes. Stir in the beef and cook until brown.

2 Add the chilli, tomatoes, sultanas (golden raisins) and cashew nuts and cook until the mixture is quite dry.

3 Remove the pan from the heat and stir in half the Parmesan cheese and the seasoning.

4 Place the paw-paw (papaya) shells in a shallow ovenproof dish and spoon the beef mixture into the shells.

5 Pour boiling water into the dish to come a quarter of the way up the paw-paws (papayas). Mix the remaining cheese with the breadcrumbs and sprinkle over the paw-paws (papayas). Bake in a preheated oven at 180°C/350°F/Gas Mark 4 for 30 minutes.

6 Carefully lift the paw-paws (papayas) from the dish with a perforated spoon. Garnish with flat-leaf parsley and serve.

STEP 2

STEP 4

VARIATION

Ring the changes by using (bell) peppers in place of paw-paws (papayas); slice in half through the stalks, remove the seeds, and fill and bake in the same way.

STEP 5

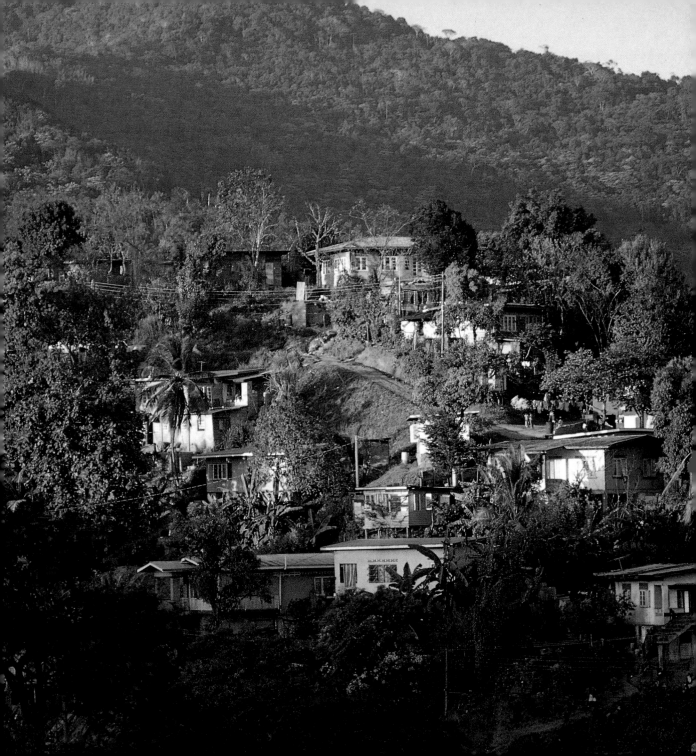

CHAPTER FOUR

Vegetables & Salads

West Indians love vegetables, so there will be at least two vegetable accompaniments at every main meal. Many of the exotic vegetables are now available in supermarkets, markets and specialist stores. Some of the vegetables may look rather unfamiliar to you, but they are simple to prepare and are used in much the same way as more traditional vegetables. Regularly used vegetables include sweet potato, breadfruit, cho-cho, okra, paw-paw (papaya), plantain, callaloo, yam, eddo and a selection of beans.

Salads are also eaten regularly but are served as accompaniments rather than a main dish. They usually consist of one or more ingredients, such as potatoes, okra, tomatoes, onions, beans, callaloo, nuts and tropical fruits. Salads are dressed in a spicy or well seasoned dressing or sauce. Whatever pepper sauce you are using to prepare a dish, remember to place a bowl or bottle of it on the table so each person can drizzle extra over their own dishes, as is the custom on the islands.

Opposite: *Houses nestling amongst the dense vegetation on the hillsides of Port of Spain, Trinidad.*

STEP 1

STEP 2

STEP 4

STEP 7

BREADFRUIT COO-COO

The word 'coo-coo' means a cooked side dish. This recipe is traditionally credited to Barbados, though it turns up in various forms in a great many of the islands. It makes a good accompaniment to many meat, poultry or fish dishes.

SERVES 6

1 kg/2 lb breadfruit, or a 760 g/25 oz can
250 g/8 oz salt beef, chopped finely
1 onion, chopped finely
½ tsp dried thyme
1 fresh bay leaf
1 sprig fresh parsley
3 fresh chive stalks
125 g/4 oz/½ cup unsalted butter
2 tbsp olive oil
salt and pepper

TO GARNISH:
cherry tomatoes
sprigs of fresh parsley

1 Peel the breadfruit, cut out the core and roughly chop the flesh. If using canned breadfruit, drain and chop coarsely. Place in a saucepan with the salt beef and onion.

2 Wrap the thyme, bay leaf, parsley and chives in a piece of muslin (cheesecloth) and add to the pan with enough cold water to cover. Bring to the boil, cover and simmer for 25–30 minutes until the breadfruit is tender.

3 Drain, reserving the liquid, and return the ingredients to the pan.

Discard the muslin (cheesecloth) bag.

4 Mash half the butter into the pan, adding a little of the reserved liquid if necessary to make a smooth but slightly stiff consistency like mashed potatoes. Season to taste.

5 Butter a shallow dish and turn the breadfruit mixture into it. Smooth down and refrigerate for a few hours.

6 Turn out on to a lightly floured surface and cut into triangles.

7 Heat the remaining butter with the oil in a large frying pan (skillet) and fry the triangles a few at a time for 2–3 minutes on each side until golden. Remove with a perforated spoon and drain on paper towels. Garnish with cherry tomatoes and parsley and serve.

VARIATION

Breadfruit coo-coo may also be eaten without frying; after mashing, press it into a buttered dish, then turn out on to a warmed plate. Dot with butter and serve.

STEP 1

STEP 2

STEP 3

STEP 4

OKRA IN SPICY TOMATO SAUCE

Okra is of tropical Asian origin but was first introduced to the islands by Africans. It is now widely used on all the islands. This particular recipe originates from St Croix, one of the Leeward Islands.

SERVES 4

2 tbsp extra-virgin olive oil
1 large onion, chopped
2 garlic cloves, crushed
6 large ripe tomatoes, skinned and chopped
1 fresh red chilli, deseeded and chopped
3–4 fresh basil leaves, torn into fine shreds
large pinch of curry powder
1 tbsp tomato purée (paste)
175 ml/6 fl oz/¾ cup water
500 g/1 lb okra, trimmed
salt and pepper
fresh basil leaves, torn, to garnish

1 Heat the oil in a large saucepan, add the onion and fry for 5 minutes until soft but not brown. Add the garlic and fry for a further 2 minutes.

2 Stir in the tomatoes, chilli, basil, curry powder, tomato purée (paste), water and seasoning.

3 Bring to the boil, reduce the heat and simmer for 5 minutes.

4 Add the okra and cook for 15–20 minutes, stirring occasionally, until the okra is tender.

5 Transfer to a warmed serving dish and garnish with basil leaves.

OKRA

Okra, or ladies' fingers, is available fresh or canned. Fresh okra is available from supermarkets, while canned okra can be found in specialist stores and markets. Use a 350 g/12 oz can for this recipe; drain well and heat for 10 minutes in step 4.

STEP 2

STEP 3

STEP 4

STEP 5

RICE & PEAS

Another inter-island speciality, this dish is traditionally served with Sunday lunch. The 'peas' are red kidney beans, which are called 'peas' in Jamaica, the country with which this dish is often associated.

SERVES 6

175 g/6 oz/scant 1 cup dried red kidney beans, soaked overnight in cold water
2 tbsp groundnut oil
4 spring onions (scallions), sliced
1 small fresh red chilli, sliced
2 garlic cloves, crushed
125 g/4 oz creamed coconut, chopped
400 ml/14 fl oz/1³⁄₄ cups boiling water
1 sprig fresh thyme
500 g/1 lb/2¹⁄₂ cups long-grain rice
salt and pepper

1 Drain the beans. Rinse and place in a large saucepan with enough cold water to cover by about 5 cm/2 inches. Bring to the boil and boil rapidly for 10 minutes. Reduce the heat to simmering and cook, covered, for 1–1¹⁄₂ hours until the beans are almost tender.

2 Drain the beans, reserving the cooking liquid. Make the liquid up to 500 ml/16 fl oz/2 cups with cold water if necessary.

3 Return the beans and liquid to the saucepan.

4 Heat the oil in a frying pan (skillet) and fry the spring onions (scallions), chilli and garlic for 1–2 minutes. Add to the beans.

5 Dissolve the creamed coconut in the boiling water. Stir into the pan with the thyme, rice and seasoning. Cover and cook over a very low heat for about 20 minutes until the rice and beans are tender and all the liquid has been absorbed. Discard the thyme sprigs and transfer to a warmed serving dish. Serve with meat or chicken.

VARIATION

Fresh or canned gungo (pigeon) peas are often used in this dish in place of red kidney beans.

KIDNEY BEANS

Kidney beans, also known as red peas, must be soaked, boiled and simmered according to the recipe to remove the poisonous toxins they contain. A 425 g/ 14 oz can of beans may be used for this recipe; do not cook them beforehand, simply add them with the rice.

CHEESE-STUFFED YAM BALLS

These unusual yam balls can be served as an accompaniment, or they can be eaten by themselves as a snack or with drinks.

STEP 1

MAKES 18

1 kg/2 lb yams, chopped coarsely
60 g/2 oz/¼ cup butter
2 eggs, beaten
2 spring onions (scallions), chopped
125 g/4 oz Mozzarella or Edam cheese, cut
  into 18 cubes
18 pimento-stuffed olives
175 g/6 oz/1½ cups dry fine breadcrumbs
corn oil for deep frying
salt and pepper
watercress to garnish

1 Put the yams into a large saucepan. Pour in enough cold water to cover. Bring to the boil, cover and simmer for 15 minutes until soft. Drain well and add the butter, half the eggs and the seasoning. Mash with a potato masher to a smooth purée. Mix in the spring onions (scallions).

2 Shape the mixture into 18 balls. Push a piece of cheese and an olive into the centre of each ball and reshape the yam mixture around them.

3 Roll the yam balls in the remaining egg, then in the breadcrumbs until coated on all sides.

4 Heat the oil in a deep-fat fryer or saucepan to 190°C/375°F or until a cube of bread turns brown in 40 seconds. Deep-fry the yam balls in batches for about 2 minutes until golden brown. Remove with a perforated spoon and drain on paper towels. Keep warm while frying the remaining balls.

5 Place on a warm serving plate and garnish with watercress.

STEP 2

STEP 3

YAMS

Yams have a flavour similar to potatoes although the yam is slightly nuttier. Potatoes or sweet potatoes may be used in this recipe instead.

STEP 4

STEP 1

STEP 2

STEP 3

STEP 4

STUFFED CHO-CHO

Tropical cho-chos, or christophenes, belong to the tropical squash family and have a taste much like the summer squash. This dish is good for vegetarians, as it makes a filling main meal.

SERVES 6

3 large cho-chos, each weighing about 350 g/12 oz
60 g/2 oz/¼ cup butter
1 large Spanish onion, chopped
1 large red (bell) pepper, chopped
3 spring onions (scallions), sliced
350 g/12 oz/3 cups cashew nuts, toasted
125 g/4 oz/2 cups fresh breadcrumbs
1 egg, lightly beaten
125 g/4 oz/1 cup mature (sharp) Cheddar cheese, grated
1 fresh green chilli, chopped
salt and pepper

TO GARNISH:
sprigs of fresh parsley
fresh red chillies

1 Cook the whole cho-chos in boiling salted water for 30 minutes until tender. Drain and leave until cool enough to handle. Halve lengthways. Scoop out the pulp, including the edible seed (pit), and set aside. Arrange the shells in a shallow ovenproof dish.

2 Heat half the butter in a frying pan (skillet), add the cho-cho pulp, the onion and (bell) pepper and cook for 5 minutes. Stir in the spring onions (scallions) and cook for a further 2 minutes, stirring frequently.

3 Add the cashews, breadcrumbs, egg, cheese, chilli and seasoning and stir well.

4 Pack into the cho-cho shells, dot with the remaining butter and bake in a preheated oven at 180°C/350°F/Gas Mark 4 for 15 minutes until lightly browned.

5 Transfer to a warmed serving plate, garnish with parsley and red chillies and serve.

VARIATION

Courgettes (zucchini) and marrow may also be stuffed and cooked in this way.

STEP 1

STEP 3

STEP 4

STEP 5

CARIBBEAN YAM SALAD

Salads are an important part of a West Indian meal. The ingredients are always varied and generally quite spicy.

SERVES 6

750 g/1½ lb yam, unpeeled
¼ cucumber, peeled and chopped
2 hard-boiled (hard-cooked) eggs, quartered
8 cherry tomatoes, halved
2 dill pickles, sliced
3 spring onions (scallions), sliced
2 celery sticks, sliced
1 tbsp chopped fresh chives
1 tsp paprika
salt and pepper
celery leaves to garnish

DRESSING:
150 ml/¼ pint/⅔ cup mayonnaise
4 tbsp natural fromage frais
2 tbsp white wine vinegar
1 tsp finely grated lemon rind

1 To make the dressing, mix together the mayonnaise, fromage frais, vinegar, lemon rind and seasoning. Chill until required.

2 Place the yam in a large saucepan, cover with water and bring to the boil. Cook for 20–25 minutes until tender. Drain and leave until cool enough to handle.

3 Peel the yam and cut into 2.5 cm/ 1 inch cubes.

4 Place the yam in a bowl and pour over the dressing. Mix well to coat.

5 Carefully fold in the cucumber, eggs, tomatoes, dill pickles, spring onions (scallions), celery, chives and paprika. Adjust the seasoning.

6 Spoon into a serving bowl, cover and refrigerate for at least 1 hour. Serve garnished with celery leaves.

VARIATION

Cooked meats, such as shredded chicken, chopped ham or beef, may be added to this salad for a more substantial meal.

CHAPTER FIVE

Desserts & Cakes

The sweet-toothed islanders love puddings, buns and cakes, which is hardly surprising since the islands are overflowing with luscious fruits and sugar cane. Desserts tend to be very sweet, alcoholic or fruity, and usually a combination of all three. Any alcohol used is usually locally produced rum, which is traditionally kept in the store cupboard along with canned cream and condensed and evaporated milks because fresh milk and cream are unavailable on most of the islands.

Much use is made of the local fruits in all kinds of desserts, especially mouthwatering ice creams. The principal fruits include bananas, mangoes, paw-paws (papayas), guavas, pineapples, soursops and limes. Even ingredients which are normally associated with savoury dishes, such as cornmeal, sweet potato and breadfruit, are sometimes used in desserts.

Moist, rich cakes, sweet breads and buns are very popular. Cakes and buns are often served with wedges of cheese at breakfast, lunch or supper. Common ingredients include coconut, dried fruits, spices and, of course, a dash of local rum.

Opposite: *The climate of the Caribbean ensures a year-round supply of colourful, mouthwatering fruits.*

STEP 1

STEP 2

STEP 4

STEP 5

TROPICAL FRUIT ICE CREAMS

*Mouthwatering ice cream is particularly popular in the Caribbean, and
with such a variety of tropical fruits the variations are almost limitless.
Cooks on the island of Grenada have a simple recipe: make one basic
custard and add whichever puréed fruit you like.*

SERVES 6–8

4 eggs
*125 g/4 oz/1¼ cups caster (superfine)
    sugar*
250 ml/8 fl oz/1 cup single (light) cream
125 ml/¼ pint/⅔ cup milk
125 ml/¼ pint/⅔ cup evaporated milk
½ tsp vanilla flavouring (extract)
*125 g/4 oz/½ cup canned crushed
    pineapple, drained*
175 g/6 oz/¾ cup caster (superfine) sugar
*125 g/4 oz/½ cup puréed canned or ripe
    paw-paw (papaya)*
1 tbsp lemon juice
sprigs of fresh mint to decorate

SOURSOP ICE CREAM:
450 ml/¾ pint/2 cups canned soursop juice
*300 ml/½ pint/1½ cups double (heavy)
    cream*
90 g/3oz/⅓ cup caster (superfine) sugar

1 Beat the eggs with the sugar in a
large heatproof bowl. Heat the
cream, milk and evaporated milk to
scalding point. Stir the milk mixture into
the eggs.

2 Place the bowl over a saucepan
half-filled with simmering water.
Cook over a low heat, stirring constantly,
until the mixture is thick enough to coat
the back of a spoon. Leave to cool, then
stir in the vanilla flavouring (extract).

3 Pour half the custard into another
bowl. Add the pineapple and
125 g/4 oz/½ cup of the sugar to one
bowl and the paw-paw (papaya),
remaining sugar and lemon juice to the
other bowl. Stir until the sugar dissolves.

4 Pour into separate freezerproof
containers and freeze for 2–3 hours
until just becoming firm. Remove from
the freezer and beat well. Return to the
containers and freeze until frozen.

5 To make the soursop ice cream,
mix the soursop juice with the
double (heavy) cream and sugar. Freeze
as in step 4.

6 Remove the ice creams from the
freezer 1 hour before serving and
place in the refrigerator, to allow the ice
creams to soften slightly. Decorate with
mint sprigs and serve.

STEP 1

STEP 2

STEP 3

STEP 4

FLAMED BAKED BANANAS

Bananas are used extensively throughout the Caribbean and appear in many recipes. This simple but impressive dessert from Antigua never fails to impress when it is brought, still flaming, to the table.

SERVES 4

125 g/4 oz/¹/₂ cup unsalted butter
4 large ripe bananas, halved lengthways
250 g/8 oz/1¹/₃ cups soft light brown sugar
120 ml/4 fl oz/¹/₂ cup orange juice
250 ml/8 fl oz/1 cup white rum
2 tsp ground allspice
double (heavy) cream, lightly whipped, to
  serve
orange shreds to decorate (see page 72)

1 Use a little of the butter to grease a shallow ovenproof dish. Arrange the banana halves in a single layer in the dish.

2 Sprinkle with the sugar. Mix together the orange juice, half the rum and the allspice. Pour over the bananas.

3 Dot the bananas with the remaining buttter. Bake in a preheated oven at 200°C/400°F/Gas Mark 6 for 15 minutes, basting halfway through.

4 Remove the bananas from the oven and transfer to a flameproof serving dish, if wished. Warm the remaining rum in a small saucepan.

5 Top the bananas with whipped cream and decorate with orange shreds. Pour over the warmed rum and carefully set alight. Serve as soon as the flames have died down. If preferred, the bananas can be flamed in the baking dish, then transferred to serving dishes and decorated when the flames die down.

VARIATION

You can vary the flavour of the sauce in this dish by using lime or lemon juice instead of orange juice. Add another 30 g/1 oz/2 tablespoons sugar as these fruits are sharper than oranges. Remember to decorate with lime or lemon shreds, made as the orange shreds on page 72.

STEP 1

STEP 2

STEP 3

STEP 5

LIME MERINGUE PIE

Most Caribbean cooks have a recipe for lime meringue pie. It is a popular dessert, especially after Sunday lunch.

SERVES 6

3 tbsp cornflour (cornstarch)
150 ml/¼ pint/⅔ cup water
grated rind and juice of 4 limes
125 g/4 oz/½ cup caster (superfine) sugar
2 egg yolks
lime slices to decorate

MERINGUE:
2 egg whites
60 g/2 oz/¼ cup caster (superfine) sugar

PASTRY:
125 g/4 oz/1 cup plain (all-purpose) flour
60 g/2 oz/¼ cup butter, diced
about 1½ tbsp cold water

1 To make the pastry, sift the flour into a bowl, add the butter and rub in until the mixture resembles fine breadcrumbs. Mix in enough cold water to form a soft but not sticky dough. Wrap in clingfilm (plastic wrap) and refrigerate for 15 minutes.

2 Knead the pastry lightly then roll out and use to line a deep 20 cm/ 8 inch flan tin (quiche pan). Line with foil, weight with baking beans and bake at 200°C/400°F/Gas Mark 6 for 10–15 minutes. Remove the foil and beans and

bake for a further 5 minutes. Reduce the oven temperature to 180°C/350°F/Gas Mark 4.

3 Mix the cornflour (cornstarch) with the water and lime rind and juice, put in a saucepan and bring slowly to the boil, stirring until the mixture thickens. Add the sugar.

4 Remove from the heat and cool slightly. Add the egg yolks and cook over a low heat, stirring constantly, for 2–3 minutes; do not allow to boil. Pour into the pastry case.

5 To make the meringue, whisk the egg whites until stiff, then whisk in half the sugar until soft peaks form. Fold in the remaining sugar.

6 Spread the meringue on top of the pie and bake for 10–15 minutes until the meringue is lightly browned. Serve hot or cold, decorated with lime slices.

GINGER & COCONUT BREAD

The addition of coconut gives this traditional Jamaican gingerbread a new twist. Store in an airtight container for up to two weeks – the longer it is kept the more moist it becomes.

STEP 1

MAKES 1 KG/2 LB LOAF

300 g/10 oz/2¹/₂ cups plain (all-purpose) flour
2 tsp baking powder
2 tsp ground ginger
1 tsp bicarbonate of soda (baking soda)
1 tsp ground allspice
60 g/2 oz/²/₃ cup unsweetened desiccated (shredded) coconut
125 g/4 oz/²/₃ cup soft dark brown sugar
175 g/6 oz/³/₄ cup dark molasses
125 g/4 oz/¹/₂ cup unsalted butter
175 ml/6 fl oz/³/₄ cup evaporated milk
2 eggs, beaten
2 tbsp sieved warmed apricot jam
fresh coconut shreds to decorate (optional)

1 Lightly grease and line the bottom of a 1 kg/2 lb loaf tin (pan). Sift the flour, baking powder, ground ginger, bicarbonate of soda (baking soda) and allspice into a large bowl. Stir in the coconut.

2 Place the sugar, molasses and butter in a saucepan and heat gently until the butter has melted and the molasses and sugar dissolved. Remove from the heat, leave to cool, then stir in the evaporated milk and eggs and mix well.

3 Pour into the flour and coconut mixture and mix well. Pour into the loaf tin (pan) and bake in a preheated oven at 170°C/325°F/Gas Mark 3 for 50 minutes until a skewer inserted into the centre comes out clean.

4 Allow to cool in the tin (pan). Turn out and brush the top with the jam. Slice and serve as it is, or spread with butter, and decorated with coconut, if liked.

STEP 2

STEP 3

MOLASSES

A by-product of sugar-making, this syrup is available as dark and light and improves the keeping qualities of bread and cakes.

COCONUT SHREDS

To make coconut shreds, use a potato peeler to 'peel' strips from the flesh of a fresh coconut.

STEP 4

STEP 1

STEP 2

STEP 3

STEP 4

ORANGE TEACAKE

This is a popular cake in Barbados and many of the English-speaking islands. It is so tangy and moist it will disappear in next to no time.

Makes 1 kg/2 lb loaf

250 g/8 oz/2 cups plain (all-purpose) flour
2 tsp baking powder
½ tsp salt
125 g/4 oz/½ cup caster (superfine) sugar
1 tbsp finely grated orange rind
2 eggs, beaten
250 ml/8 fl oz/1 cup orange juice, strained
45 g/1½ oz/3 tbsp unsalted butter, melted
orange shreds to decorate

1 Grease and line the bottom of a 1 kg/2 lb loaf tin (pan). Sift the flour, baking powder and salt into a bowl. Stir in the sugar and orange rind.

2 In a separate bowl, whisk together the eggs, orange juice and butter.

3 Carefully fold the egg mixture into the dry ingredients.

4 Pour into the loaf tin (pan) and bake in a preheated oven at 180°C/350°F/Gas Mark 4 for 45 minutes until a skewer inserted in the centre comes out clean.

5 Allow to cool in the tin (pan) for 10 minutes. Turn out on to a wire rack and leave to cool.

6 Serve sliced, decorated with orange shreds. Store any remaining cake in an airtight container.

ORANGE SHREDS

For perfect orange shreds, use a cannelle knife to peel away thin strips of rind from the fruit, taking care not to include any bitter pith. Alternatively, use a potato peeler to peel off the rind. Slice very finely into shreds, blanch in boiling water for 1 minute and refresh under cold water.

VARIATION

Try using lemon or lime rind and juice for a lemon or lime teacake. Decorate with lemon or lime shreds, as above.

STEP 2

STEP 3

STEP 5

STEP 7

JAMAICAN SPICED BUNS

Jamaican bun is a spicy, dried fruit bun that is often served at breakfast time. The bun is usually sliced and eaten with cheese. This recipe for individual buns is an adaptation of a traditional recipe.

MAKES 12–14

275 g/9 oz/generous cup butter or
  margarine, melted
150 g/5 oz/scant 1 cup soft light brown
  sugar
1 egg, beaten
500 g/1 lb/4 cups strong plain (all-
  purpose) flour
60 g/2 oz fast-action dried yeast
275 g/9 oz/1¹⁄₂ cups mixed dried fruit
2 tsp ground allspice
¹⁄₂ tsp vanilla flavouring (extract)
2 tbsp dark molasses
150 ml/5 fl oz/²⁄₃ cup milk
pinch of salt

GLAZE:
3 tbsp caster (superfine) sugar
3 tbsp water

1 Mix together the butter or margarine, sugar and egg. Sift the flour and salt and stir in the yeast.

2 Stir the butter mixture, dried fruit, allspice, vanilla and molasses into the flour mixture and gradually stir in the milk. Mix well.

3 Knead into a soft dough, then place in a clean, lightly oiled bowl. Cover with a damp cloth and leave to rise in a warm place for about 2 hours until doubled in volume.

4 Turn out the dough and knock back (punch down). Knead again on a lightly floured work surface for about 10 minutes until smooth.

5 Divide the dough into 12–14 pieces and shape into small buns using the palm of the hand. Lightly oil and flour a baking sheet and put the buns on it, spaced well apart. Leave to rise in a warm place for about 30 minutes.

6 Bake in a preheated oven at 190°C/375°F/Gas Mark 5 for 30 minutes until golden and firm to the touch.

7 To make the sugar glaze, put the sugar and water in a small saucepan, bring to the boil and boil for 2 minutes. Brush over the buns while they are still warm. Cool on a wire rack. Serve warm or cold, split and buttered and accompanied by a slice of cheese if liked.

CARIBBEAN COOKING

DRINKS
Freshly squeezed fruit juices and tropical punches are popular on the islands. Here are a few recipes to quench your thirst.

Rum Punch

350 ml/12 fl oz/1½ cups dark rum
120 ml/4 fl oz/½ cup freshly squeezed lime juice
250 ml/8 fl oz/1 cup Sugar Syrup (see page 78)
500 ml/16 fl oz/2 cups water
few drops of Angostura bitters
freshly grated nutmeg (optional)

Stir the rum, lime juice, sugar syrup and water together. Pour into glasses, add a drop of Angostura bitters to each glass and a pinch of nutmeg, if liked.

Pina Colada

500 ml/16 fl oz/2 cups pineapple juice
250 ml/8 fl oz/1 cup coconut milk
250 ml/8 fl oz/1 cup white rum
crushed ice to serve
pineapple slices to decorate

Place the pineapple juice, coconut milk and rum in a cocktail shaker or large screw-top jar. Shake vigorously. Pour into glasses containing crushed ice. Decorate with fresh pineapple if liked.

HISTORY OF CARIBBEAN CUISINE
There are over 200 islands in the Caribbean, including the Greater Antilles (Cuba, Jamaica, Haiti and Puerto Rico), the smaller islands of the Lesser Antilles, the Leeward and Windward Islands and the Virgin Islands. The turbulent history of this area has left its mark on the culture, customs and, most importantly, the food and cooking. Caribbean cuisine has been influenced by peoples from Europe, India, Africa and China and over the years these influences have combined with the native foods to create a cuisine that is quite unique. The word 'creole' is often used with reference to Caribbean food – the term indicates a dish with mixed African and European influence.

The Amerindians
The food of the islands owes much to the native Amerindians – the Arawak – who cultivated crops such as chillies, corn, garlic, yams, sweet potatoes, pineapples, guava and cassava, and made spices by grinding berries, leaves and buds. They concocted a preservative from cassava and added it to a meat and chilli stew that is still eaten throughout the islands today, and known as Pepperpot. The Arawak also preserved meat by rubbing in spices and chillies then cooking it slowly over a fire until the meat was dry but full of flavour. This method of cooking, or barbecuing (an Arawak word), was adopted by the Mexicans and the West Indians, who described food cooked in this way as 'jerky'. Although the need to preserve meat has disappeared, the tenderizing and flavouring qualities are still popular and jerked dishes are now the very essence of Caribbean cooking – they have even become popular as a fast food.

Colonial influences
Slaves from the west coast of Africa were brought to the islands in the seventeenth century to work on the sugar cane plantations. They brought with them okra, greens such as callaloo, black-eyed peas (beans) and pigeon peas.

Of the many European nations that colonized the islands in the seventeenth and eighteenth centuries, the most influential were the British, Spanish and French, who brought with them foodstuffs from all over the world. The British brought Worcestershire sauce and rum; the French introduced herbs such as chives as well as some of the more complex cooking techniques; from the Spanish came onions, sugar cane, oranges, bananas and limes. It was also the Europeans who first introduced salted fish and meats, which were used to feed the slaves.

As the islands frequently changed hands, the cooking of any one island and the names of the local dishes can be seen to have several influences. Jamaica's Caveached Fish, for example, comes from the Spanish dish known as *escabeche*, and Sancoche started life as the South American *sancocho*. But it was the last controlling power of each island that really left its mark. Flamed Baked Bananas is a typical French dish from Martinique; the British influence in Jamaica can be seen in the Jamaican Patty – a spiced meat parcel that is a descendant of the Cornish pasty; the cuisine of India is reflected in the curries and roti (a type of flat bread) of Trinidad, and in their use of ghee.

Island specialities
Despite the colonial influences, many dishes and ingredients are shared by more than one island, although they often have different names, and recipes may contain slightly different ingredients. On some islands, for example, avocado is known as zaboca; christophene is chayote or cho-cho; and salt-fish fritters are called 'Stamp and Go' in Jamaica but on Martinique they are known as accra.

Ingredients are also used in diverse ways: Cubans prefer black beans although most islands used red beans; Virgin islanders use spinach instead of callaloo; in Jamaica, chillies are used to preserve foods while elsewhere they are mixed with herbs and spices to tenderize tough cuts of meat. The use of chillies for their flavour, however, is widespread and on all the islands they are added to marinades, rubs, sauces, curries, stews and salads. Cakes and desserts made from coconuts or bananas are also popular.

CARIBBEAN TECHNIQUES
Seasoning-up or marinating meats, fish and poultry is essential to authentic Caribbean dishes, although basic ingredients can be altered according to personal taste. The range of seasoning ingredients available is so vast that most cooks vary them every time they cook.

Caribbean cooks are quite fastidious about the appearance of a finished dish, so herbs that will leave specks in a sauce are often tied in muslin (cheesecloth) before being added to the pot.

Whole chillies, with the stem left on, are sometimes added to the pot to impart their flavour without the heat. They should be removed before serving. Chopped chillies may also be tied in muslin (cheesecloth).

Many recipes use fresh herbs, as their flavour is so much better than that of dried ones. Fresh herbs need not always be chopped first, sometimes the stems are crushed, to release the flavour, then the whole sprig added to the pot. The sprig should be removed before serving.

COOKING EQUIPMENT
No specialist equipment is required. For best results, use good quality, heavy-based pans. Casseroles that are both flameproof and ovenproof are a good choice. As many creole dishes contain acids such as vinegar or lime or lemon juice, use non-metallic dishes and pans that have a non-metallic coating, as the acid can react with the metal.

THE SPIRIT OF CARIBBEAN COOKING
Caribbean cooking comes from the soul, and most dishes have an informal, home-made feel without any fancy techniques or ingredients, relying more on the overall look, feel and flavour of a dish. Most islanders use recipes that have been handed down through the generations;

Carrot Juice

280 g/9 oz/1¹/₂ cups finely grated carrots
1 litre/1³/₄ pints/4 cups water
425 g/14 oz can condensed milk
180 ml/6 fl oz/³/₄ cup evaporated milk
dash of Angostura bitters
crushed ice to serve
freshly grated nutmeg or cinnamon (optional) to decorate

Mix the carrots with the water. Leave to stand for at least 30 minutes. Press through a sieve (strainer). Stir the condensed and evaporated milks into the carrot juice and add a dash of Angostura bitters. Chill. Pour into glasses containing crushed ice and sprinkle with nutmeg or cinnamon if liked.

Tropical Fruit Punch

1 large mango or paw-paw (papaya)
300 ml/¹/₂ pint/1¹/₄ cups fresh orange juice
300 ml/¹/₂ pint/1¹/₄ cups pineapple juice
150 ml/¹/₄ pint/²/₃ cup fresh lime juice
4 tbsp Sugar Syrup (see page 78)
4 tsp grenadine
crushed ice to serve
orange and pineapple slices to decorate

Purée the mango or paw-paw (papaya) in a food processor or blender until smooth. Alternatively, press through a non-metallic sieve (strainer).

Transfer to a large jug and stir in the orange juice, pineapple juice, lime juice and sugar syrup. Pour into glasses containing crushed ice and add 1 teaspoon of grenadine to each. Decorate with orange and pineapple slices.

Sugar Syrup
This syrup gives a smoother taste to drinks and can be used in place of sugar. One tablespoon is equivalent to 1½ teaspoons of sugar.

500 g/1 lb/2 cups granulated sugar
450 ml/¾ pint/2 cups cold water

Stir the sugar and water together until the sugar dissolves. Pour into a plastic container or screw-top jar and refrigerate until required.

GHEE
Slowly melt 500 g/1 lb/2 cups diced butter in a heavy-based saucepan, stirring occasionally. Bring to the boil and boil for 1 minute. Reduce the heat to the lowest setting and cook without stirring for 45 minutes. Line a sieve (strainer) with muslin (cheesecloth) that has been soaked in hot water and wrung out. Strain the butter through the muslin (cheesecloth). Seal and keep refrigerated.

recipes and quantities are used only for guidance and most cooks add their own secret ingredients or special touches to their favourite dishes. The basic rule of this unique, exotic cuisine is to be inventive and not afraid of adapting the recipes to suit your own tastes. Spice them up and down as you feel and vary the ingredients according to what is available, but above all, enjoy it!

CARIBBEAN INGREDIENTS
As people from the Caribbean now live all over the world, ingredients that were once unheard of outside the area are quite widely available. You should be able to find all of the following in street markets, ethnic stores or large supermarkets.

Ackee, akee, achee
This fruit is used as a vegetable in Jamaica and served with salt cod. It is dark red on the outside and has creamy white flesh with shiny black seeds. Only the flesh should be eaten as the seeds, skin and pink membrane are poisonous.

Avocado
Known in Trinidad as zaboca and in other parts of the Caribbean as alligator pear, midshipman's butter or guacate. To test the ripeness, apply gentle pressure to the top – if it yields, it is ready for use.

Bananas & banana leaves
Both green and ripe bananas are used in vast quantities and are one of the main exports of the Caribbean. Green bananas are used as a vegetable. Foods are sometimes wrapped in banana leaves before cooking, which gives the food a delicate flavour.

Breadfruit
Breadfruit is a large fruit with mottled, green, rough skin and a yellowish white flesh. It is not edible until it has been cooked. It tastes like potato with a slightly nutty flavour, and can be boiled, fried, roasted or barbecued and served in salads, soups, stews or as fritters. When buying, look for firm, heavy fruit.

Callaloo
The West Indian and Creole name for the tops of the taro plant, or Caribbean spinach. The leaves are used like spinach.

Cho-cho, christophene or chayote
This pear-shaped, pale green, slightly prickly squash has a single edible seed (pit) and white flesh with a delicate flavour. It is usually boiled or fried then stuffed and baked. Also available canned.

Coconut milk
Cans of coconut milk are available in ethnic stores and supermarkets. Creamed coconut, which comes in the form of a solid bar, can be grated or chopped and mixed with water to give coconut milk.

Cornmeal
Cornmeal is ground corn. It can be made into porridge (or 'pap', as it is known), puddings, bread or dumplings.

Ghee
Ghee is a type of clarified butter which can be heated to much higher temperatures than ordinary butter.

Herbs & spices

Many of the herbs and spices used in Caribbean cooking are now grown in abundance and exported all over the world, so they are quite easy to find.

Mango

The skin of ripe mangoes varies in colour from green to a deep rose red and the flesh from pale yellow to bright orange. The fruit is ripe when the flesh yields to a gentle pressure.

Okra, ochro, ladies' fingers, bamie

Okra is a green, slightly hairy pod that is available fresh or canned. It is served as an accompaniment, or added to stews and soups for its thickening qualities as well as its flavour.

Paw-paw (papaya)

This elongated, pear-shaped fruit is hard and green when unripe, when it is used as a vegetable in chutneys and relishes. When ripe it has a yellow to orange skin. The seeds are edible but have a peppery taste. It is available fresh and canned.

Peppers & chillies

Sweet peppers, also known as bell peppers or capsicums, and hot chillies characterize all island cooking. The chilli peppers are among the hottest in the world and are used in many sauces and relishes. They are sometimes available crushed and preserved in vinegar or as bottled sauces. Scotch bonnet chillies, which are small and lantern-shaped, are very hot indeed. The seeds of a chilli are the hottest part, so remove them if you don't want your dish to be too fiery.

Plantain

Plantains are a member of the banana family, but must be cooked before eating. They look like large green bananas and are usually used when unripe (green).

Rice

This is the staple diet of the islands and forms the basis of most meals. Use good-quality long-grain rice.

Soursop

Soursop is a large, heart-shaped, spiny, dark green fruit. When opened, it has an edible white pulp with black seeds. Soursop has a refreshing taste and is used mainly in ices, drinks and sherbets. It is available canned.

Sweet potato

The skin colour of this root vegetable is reddish brown, pink or white. The flesh ranges from deep orange through yellow to white. Although it is a vegetable, it is used in both sweet and savoury dishes. The sweet potato is very versatile and can be boiled, roasted, fried, or cooked over a barbecue.

Yam

This root vegetable has a bark-like skin, creamy yellow flesh and a nutty flavour. It is cooked in the same way as potatoes.

Yard-long beans

Yard-long beans are also known as Chinese beans and asparagus beans. These delicately flavoured narrow beans can grow up to 100 cm/40 inches long. They are available from Caribbean and Chinese food stores.

ACCOMPANIMENTS

Cornmeal Dumplings

These dumplings may also be cooked in a soup or stew.

MAKES 24

125 g/4 oz/1 cup plain (all-purpose) flour
125 g/4 oz/scant 1 cup fine cornmeal
1 tsp baking powder
1 tsp finely chopped fresh chives
45 g/1 1/2 oz/3 tbsp lard or white vegetable fat (shortening)
about 6 tbsp water
salt

Put the flour, cornmeal, baking powder, chives and a pinch of salt in a bowl. Rub in the fat until the mixture resembles fine breadcrumbs. Stir in enough water to make a stiff dough. Roll into 24 balls. Place in a pan of boiling salted water. Reduce the heat, cover and simmer for 10–15 minutes. Drain and serve.

Hot Pepper Relish

125 g/4 oz fresh red chillies, chopped
1 onion, chopped finely
salt and pepper

Put the chillies and onion in a small saucepan and cook gently for 20–30 minutes, stirring occasionally. Add a little water if it becomes too dry. Season and leave to cool. Use sparingly.

INDEX